Find the Series in the IRC	
D 545 V5 D69 2011 **(St.Catharines IRC)**	The Battle of Vimy Ridge
KE 4199 B75 2012 **(St.Catharines IRC**	Bringing Home the Constitution
FC 478 D69 2011	The British North America Act
HQ 1455 A3 D69 2011	The Famous Five
HE 2810 C2 L36 2012	The Last Spike in the CPR
PZ 7.7 G68 Te 2013 **(St. Catharines IRC)**	The Terry Fox run

DEFINING MOMENTS IN CANADIAN HISTORY

THE LAST SPIKE
IN THE CPR

Fraser River

Savona Kamloops

Yale (B.C.)

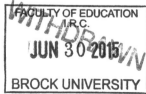
Moose Jaw

Weigl

Winnipeg Thunder Bay

Published by Weigl Educational Publishers Limited
6325 10th Street SE
Calgary, Alberta T2H 2Z9
Website: www.weigl.ca

All of the Internet URLs given in the book were valid at the time of publication. However, due to the
dynamic nature of the Internet, some addresses may have changed, or sites may have ceased to exist
since publication. While the author and publisher regret any inconvenience this may cause readers,
no responsibility for any such changes can be accepted by either the author or the publisher.

Library and Archives Canada Cataloguing in Publication

Dooling, Sandra
    The last spike in the CPR / Sandra Dooling.

(Defining moments in Canadian history)
Includes index.
ISBN 978-1-77071-689-6

    1. Canadian Pacific Railway Company--History--19th
century--Juvenile literature. 2. Railroads--Canada--History--
19th century--Juvenile literature. I. Title. II. Series: Defining
moments in Canadian history

HE2810.C2D66 2011   j385.0971   C2011-904691-1

Printed in the United States of America in North Mankato, Minnesota
1 2 3 4 5 6 7 8 9 0 15 14 13 12 11

072011
WEP040711

Senior Editor: Heather Kissock
Art Director: Terry Paulhus

Every reasonable effort has been made to trace ownership and to obtain permission to reprint
copyright material.

The publishers would be pleased to have any errors or omissions brought to their attention so that
they may be corrected in subsequent printings.

We acknowledge the financial support of the Government of Canada through the Canada Book Fund
for our publishing activities.

Contents

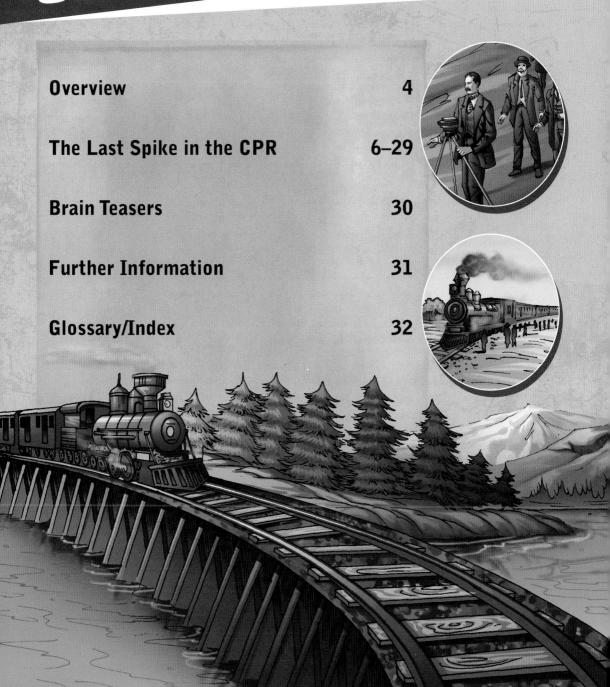

Overview

Sir John A. Macdonald recognized that Canada was a vast territory that would one day have large geographical, regional, and ethnic contrasts. He believed that a transcontinental railway would help tie the nation together. The railway would be long, stretching 5,000 kilometers. It would pass through harsh terrain, and over rugged mountains. Many people felt that the task was impossible. Macdonald, however, believed it could be done. With government help, the Canadian Pacific Railway came into being. Track was laid from the Pacific Ocean eastward and from the Great Lakes region westward. After years of work, the two lines of railway met on November 7, 1885 in Craigellachie, British Columbia. With the driving of the last **spike**, the lines were joined. Canada had its transcontinental railway.

Background Information

Sir John A. Macdonald – Leader of the Conservative Party and Canada's first and third prime minister. His dream for Canada included a transcontinental railway to bind together the various parts of the new nation.

Alexander Mackenzie – Leader of the Liberal Party, he became prime minister when the **Pacific Scandal** drove Macdonald from office. He did not favor government involvement in a transcontinental railway.

Andrew Onderdonk – An engineer and contractor from the United States, Onderdonk was hired by the government to build the western portion of the railway.

Donald A. Smith – A wealthy businessman from Winnipeg who, with his cousin George Stephen, was one of the founders of the Canadian Pacific Railway Company. He drove the final spike in the Canadian Pacific Railway.

George Stephen – A businessman from Montreal, he invested his fortune in the Canadian Pacific Railway Company. He was the first president of the CPR.

William Van Horne – Another contractor from the United States, Van Horne was hired by the newly formed Canada Pacific Railway in 1881 to oversee construction of the railway.

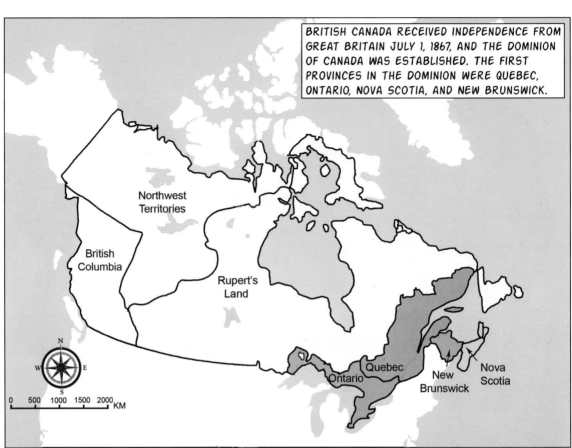

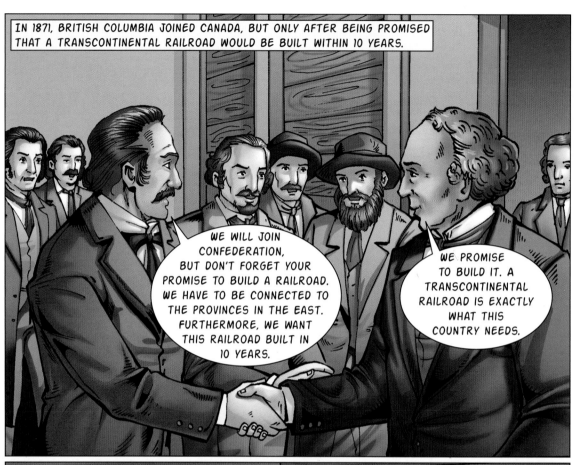

CANADIANS WERE WORRIED THAT THE UNITED STATES MIGHT TRY TO LAY CLAIM TO THE UNSETTLED LAND BETWEEN BRITISH COLUMBIA AND MANITOBA.

WE OWN THIS LAND BUT THAT MAY NOT BE ENOUGH. WE NEED TO SETTLE IT TO MAKE IT OURS.

CANADIANS HAD NOT FORGOTTEN THE CRIES OF AMERICANS TO EXTEND THEIR OREGON TERRITORY NORTHWARD TO THE 54° 40' LATITUDE LINE—ALL THE WAY UP THE PACIFIC TO RUSSIAN ALASKA. THE TREATY OF 1846 HAD SET THE BOUNDARY BETWEEN THE NATIONS, BUT IT DID NOT END ONGOING CONCERNS.

54-40 OR FIGHT

IN 1867, THE UNITED STATES BOUGHT ALASKA. WOULD THEY WANT A LAND LINK TO THEIR NEW TERRITORY?

SIR JOHN A. MACDONALD WAS THE FIRST PRIME MINISTER OF CANADA. A CONSERVATIVE, HE WAS ELECTED ON A NATIONAL POLICY PLATFORM.

THE GOVERNMENT MUST LEAD THIS NATION TO PROSPERITY. WE MUST ENCOURAGE ECONOMIC DEVELOPMENT. A TRANSCONTINENTAL RAILWAY WILL HELP ACCOMPLISH THIS.

CONSERVATIVE PARTY

HIS GOAL WAS TO BUILD A STRONG, UNITED CANADA. HE FOCUSED ON WHAT MADE CANADIANS ALIKE, NOT ON THEIR DIFFERENCES.

LET'S FOCUS ON WHAT WE HAVE IN COMMON. WE ARE ALL CANADIANS!

PRIME MINISTER MACDONALD BELIEVED THE RAILROAD THAT WAS PROMISED TO BRITISH COLUMBIA WOULD BE AN IMPORTANT WAY OF CONNECTING AND UNITING CANADA.

UNTIL THIS GREAT WORK IS COMPLETED, OUR DOMINION IS LITTLE MORE THAN A GEOGRAPHICAL EXPRESSION.

SANDFORD FLEMING WAS SENT OUT TO SURVEY A POSSIBLE ROUTE FOR THE TRANSCONTINENTAL RAILWAY. THAT ROUTE WAS DETERMINED IN 1871-1872.

SO WE'RE AGREED. THE CONTRACT FOR THE RAILROAD SHOULD GO TO SIR HUGH ALLAN.

IN 1872, THE CONSERVATIVE PARTY ACCEPTED A LARGE AMOUNT OF MONEY FROM THE MAN WHOSE COMPANY EXPECTED TO GET THE CHARTER FOR BUILDING THE RAILROAD.

NEWS TIMES

Pacific Scandal

Conservative Party accepts $350,000 in campaign funds in exchange for railway contract

WHEN THE LIBERAL PARTY FOUND OUT ABOUT THE MONEY, THEY ACCUSED MACDONALD OF ACCEPTING A BRIBE.

HOW CAN WE AS A NATION ALLOW SUCH BEHAVIOR FROM OUR ELECTED OFFICIALS?

THE PACIFIC SCANDAL DROVE MACDONALD AND HIS PARTY FROM POWER. MACDONALD RESIGNED AS PRIME MINISTER IN NOVEMBER OF 1873.

WITH THE RESIGNATION OF MACDONALD, THE CONSERVATIVES WERE REPLACED BY A LIBERAL GOVERNMENT UNDER ALEXANDER MACKENZIE. THE LIBERALS DID NOT THINK THAT THE FEDERAL GOVERNMENT SHOULD BE RESPONSIBLE FOR BUILDING A RAILWAY.

WE NEED TO FIND A PRIVATE COMPANY TO BUILD A TRANSCONTINENTAL RAILWAY. IT'S NOT THE GOVERNMENT'S JOB TO DO IT.

IT CAN BE BUILT IN STAGES. THE CONSERVATIVES WERE RECKLESS TO EXPECT THAT IT COULD BE BUILT ALL AT ONCE.

THE LIBERALS WANTED A PRIVATE COMPANY TO TAKE THE JOB. HOWEVER, THE NATION WAS EXPERIENCING A **DEPRESSION**, AND NO ONE COULD AFFORD TO BUILD A RAILWAY.

SINCE THE GOVERNMENT HAD PROMISED A RAILWAY TO BRITISH COLUMBIA, MACKENZIE KNEW THE GOVERNMENT HAD TO BUILD IT. HOWEVER, INSTEAD OF BUILDING A TRUE TRANSCONTINENTAL RAILWAY, HE DECIDED TO BUILD A FEW RAILWAYS TO LINK WATER ROUTES.

IF WE START FROM FORT WILLIAM ON THUNDER BAY, WE CAN BUILD JUST TWO SHORTER STRETCHES OF TRACK. THIS IS A MUCH MORE PRACTICAL SOLUTION THAN ONE WHOLE RAILWAY.

THIS MEANT THAT PEOPLE AND GOODS WOULD HAVE TO TRANSFER FROM RAILWAY CAR TO BOATS AND THEN BACK TO RAILWAY CARS.

IN 1875, UNDER MACKENZIE, A STRETCH OF RAILWAY WAS BUILT IN ONTARIO AT WHAT IS TODAY CALLED THUNDER BAY, ON LAKE SUPERIOR.

IN 1878, MACDONALD'S CONSERVATIVE GOVERNMENT WAS BACK IN POWER.

THE PEOPLE KNOW I WAS NEVER CONVICTED OF ANY WRONG-DOING.

I CAN'T BELIEVE THE PEOPLE OF THIS GREAT NATION PUT THAT SCOUNDREL BACK IN POWER!

WE NEED TO GET BACK TO PLANNING A REAL TRANSCONTINENTAL RAILWAY. THIS PATCHWORK OF RAIL AND WATERWAYS MY **PREDECESSOR** PLANNED IS NOT WHAT THIS COUNTRY NEEDS. IT JUST WILL NOT WORK.

IN 1879, BRITISH COLUMBIA PROPOSED SEPARATION FROM CANADA OVER THE FAILURE TO BUILD A RAILROAD.

WE MUST DO SOMETHING SOON. WE HAVE TO SHOW BRITISH COLUMBIA THAT WE WILL KEEP OUR PROMISE TO BUILD A TRANSCONTINENTAL RAILWAY.

TO PROVE ITS INTENTION OF BUILDING THE RAILWAY, THE GOVERNMENT HIRED ANDREW ONDERDONK TO BEGIN THE WESTERN PORTION OF THE LINE IN BRITISH COLUMBIA. HE WAS CONTRACTED TO LAY TRACK OVER SOME OF THE MOST DIFFICULT TERRAIN, WHICH INCLUDED FRASER CANYON.

ONDERDONK AGREED TO BUILD THE STRETCH FROM PORT MOODY TO EAGLE PASS.

THIS WILL BE AN ENGINEERING MARVEL. WE'LL HAVE TO BLAST OUR WAY THROUGH. IT WILL BE A YEAR BEFORE WE'RE READY TO LAY ANY TRACK. WE WILL NEED MEN, SUPPLIES, ROPES, **NITROGLYCERINE**. . .

FOR THE FIRST YEAR, NOT A SINGLE KILOMETER OF TRACK WAS LAID. THE TIME WAS SPENT BLASTING AWAY THE WALLS OF THE CANYON TO THE LEVEL NEEDED FOR THE RAILWAY TRACKS. WORKERS HAD TO BE LET DOWN OVER THE CANYON'S EDGE WHERE, DANGLING FROM ROPES, THEY DRILLED HOLES AND PLACED THE EXPLOSIVE CHARGES. EVEN ENGINEERS HAD TO BE LOWERED DOWN ON ROPES TO TAKE READINGS.

WHEN ALL WORKERS HAD BEEN HAULED BACK TO THE TOP, THE FUSES WERE LIT AND THE MEN RAN TO SAFETY.

SOMETIMES THE SAFETY THEY FOUND WAS NOT SAFE AT ALL. IF THE EXPLOSION WENT IN A DIFFERENT DIRECTION THAN PLANNED, ROCK COULD FLY STRAIGHT INTO THE PLACE THE MEN WERE HIDING.

SOMETIMES MORE THAN ONE EXPLOSION WAS TRIGGERED, AND MEN WERE KILLED BY THE SECOND ONE.

MISTAKES WERE FREQUENT, AND MANY MEN DIED IN THE PROCESS.

ISN'T HE THE GUY WHO FORGOT TO WASH THE NITROGLYCERINE POWDER OFF HIS HANDS BEFORE LIGHTING HIS PIPE?

HAS ANYONE SEEN JOE TODAY?

DID YOU SEE THE EXPLOSION OVER AT THE TRAILHEAD? SOME DUMMY THREW HIS BOX OF EXPLOSIVES ONTO THE PILE OF SUPPLIES!

ANDREW ONDERDONK NEEDED MASSIVE AMOUNTS OF EXPLOSIVE MATERIAL TO PREPARE THE PATH THROUGH THE MOUNTAINS, SO HE BUILT A NITROGLYCERINE FACTORY IN YALE.

FROM HERE WE CAN TAKE THE NITROGLYCERINE UP RIVER TO WHERE WE ARE BLASTING OUT THE ROADBED AND TUNNELS.

WHEN THE FACTORY BLEW UP, EVERY WINDOW IN TOWN WAS BROKEN.

ONDERDONK BUILT ANOTHER FACTORY. HIS WORKERS STILL NEEDED EXPLOSIVES IN ORDER TO BUILD THE RAILWAY.

THE BOYS UPRIVER ARE COMPLAINING THEY DON'T HAVE ENOUGH NITROGLYCERINE.

I HEARD THIS PLACE PRODUCED TWO TONS OF EXPLOSIVES A DAY.

IN ORDER TO GET SUPPLIES WHERE THEY WERE NEEDED, ONDERDONK DECIDED TO BRING A STEAMER UP THE FRASER RIVER.

THERE MUST BE AN EASIER, LESS EXPENSIVE WAY TO GET SUPPLIES TO THE UPPER FRASER RIVER. MAYBE A STEAMSHIP...

THERE WAS A **WHIRLPOOL** AT THE FOOT OF A PLACE CALLED HELL'S GATE, AND IT PRESENTED MANY DIFFICULTIES.

ONDERDONK SOLVED THEM BY HAVING WORKERS DRIVE **RING BOLTS** INTO THE WALLS OF THE UPPER FRASER RIVER CANYON AT HELL'S GATE. AFTER THREADING ROPES THROUGH THE RING BOLTS AND ATTACHING THE ROPES TO THE STEAMSHIP, THE MEN ACTUALLY PULLED THE STEAMSHIP *SKUZZY* THROUGH THE PASSAGE.

THE MOST CONTROVERSIAL STEP TAKEN BY ONDERDONK WAS THE HIRING OF CHINESE TO WORK ON THE RAILWAY. ONDERDONK HAD NOT BEEN ABLE TO FIND ENOUGH WORKERS IN BRITISH COLUMBIA, SO HE RECEIVED PERMISSION TO BRING IN CHINESE WORKERS. NOT ONLY DID THEY FILL THE GAP IN WORKERS, THEY ALSO WORKED FOR LOWER WAGES.

THEY SAY THAT ONDERDONK WENT TO THE UNITED STATES AND HIRED ALL THE CHINESE HE COULD. THEY WORKED ON THE RAILROAD IN CALIFORNIA.

HE SHOULD HAVE LEFT THEM THERE. WE DON'T NEED THEM HERE, BRINGING DOWN THE WAGES OF HARD-WORKING CANADIANS.

IN THE SPRING OF 1881, TWO BOATLOADS OF WORKERS WERE BROUGHT DIRECTLY FROM CANTON, CHINA.

MANY OF THE CHINESE DIED FROM DISEASE BEFORE REACHING THE RAILROAD CAMP. MANY OTHERS DIED WORKING ON THE RAILWAY.

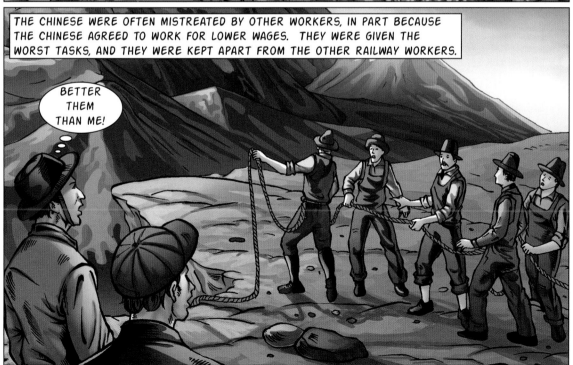

THE CHINESE WERE OFTEN MISTREATED BY OTHER WORKERS, IN PART BECAUSE THE CHINESE AGREED TO WORK FOR LOWER WAGES. THEY WERE GIVEN THE WORST TASKS, AND THEY WERE KEPT APART FROM THE OTHER RAILWAY WORKERS.

BETTER THEM THAN ME!

WHILE ONDERDONK WAS STILL PREPARING TO LAY TRACK, THE GOVERNMENT MOVED FORWARD WITH PLANS FOR THE REST OF THE RAILWAY.

WE'RE OFF TO A GOOD START IN BRITISH COLUMBIA. WE STILL NEED TO COME UP WITH A COMPANY TO BUILD AND MANAGE THE RAILROAD.

SIR, I THINK WE MAY HAVE SOME BUSINESSMEN WHO CAN DO IT.

IN 1880, A GROUP OF SCOTTISH CANADIAN BUSINESSMEN, INCLUDING GEORGE STEPHEN AND DONALD SMITH, FORMED A TRANSCONTINENTAL RAILWAY COMPANY.

I'M IMPRESSED. YOU GENTLEMEN HAVE PRACTICAL EXPERIENCE IN CONSTRUCTING AND OPERATING RAILWAYS.

OUR GROUP HAS THE RESOURCES NEEDED TO BUILD THE RAILWAY.

WE CAN PUT UP $1 MILLION AS **SECURITY** WHEN THE PLANS ARE APPROVED.

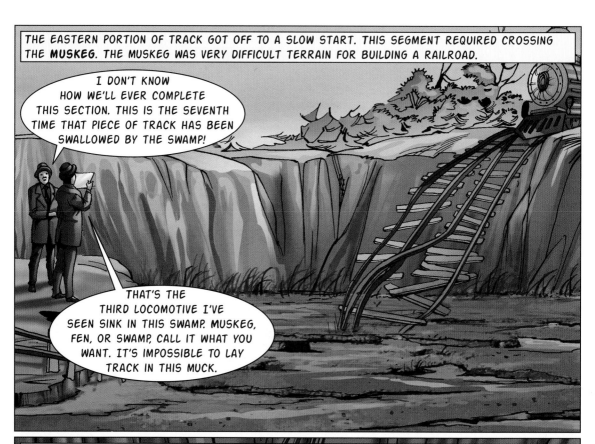

THE EASTERN PORTION OF TRACK GOT OFF TO A SLOW START. THIS SEGMENT REQUIRED CROSSING THE **MUSKEG**. THE MUSKEG WAS VERY DIFFICULT TERRAIN FOR BUILDING A RAILROAD.

I DON'T KNOW HOW WE'LL EVER COMPLETE THIS SECTION. THIS IS THE SEVENTH TIME THAT PIECE OF TRACK HAS BEEN SWALLOWED BY THE SWAMP!

THAT'S THE THIRD LOCOMOTIVE I'VE SEEN SINK IN THIS SWAMP. MUSKEG, FEN, OR SWAMP, CALL IT WHAT YOU WANT. IT'S IMPOSSIBLE TO LAY TRACK IN THIS MUCK.

TO BUILD TRACK, WORKERS HAD TO FILL THE SWAMP, CLEAR IT AWAY, OR BUILD TRESTLES TO HOLD THE TRACK. IN PLACES, THE **BEDROCK** WAS AS MUCH AS 30 METERS BELOW THE SURFACE.

I DON'T KNOW WHAT I HATE MOST: THE MUD OR THE MOSQUITOES!

NEITHER IS A BAD AS THESE BLACK FLIES!

IN 1882, THE COMPANY HIRED WILLIAM VAN HORNE TO BE THE GENERAL MANAGER. VAN HORNE HAD ALREADY PROVEN HIS ABILITIES IN THE UNITED STATES, AND HE QUICKLY APPLIED HIS SKILLS TO THE CPR.

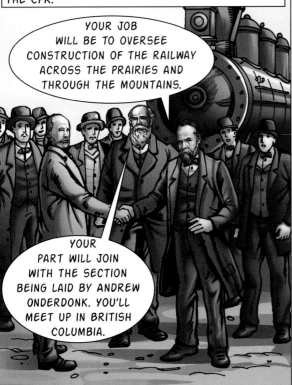

YOUR JOB WILL BE TO OVERSEE CONSTRUCTION OF THE RAILWAY ACROSS THE PRAIRIES AND THROUGH THE MOUNTAINS.

YOUR PART WILL JOIN WITH THE SECTION BEING LAID BY ANDREW ONDERDONK. YOU'LL MEET UP IN BRITISH COLUMBIA.

LAYING TRACK ACROSS THE PRAIRIES WENT MORE QUICKLY THAN IN THE MUSKEG OR THE MOUNTAINS.

DOES THIS MAN EVER SLEEP? HE HAS US LAYING TRACK ALL DAY AND NIGHT.

WE'VE GOT 5,000 MEN WORKING. THERE ARE 1,700 TEAMS OF HORSES IN USE. WE'LL MAKE GOOD PROGRESS THIS YEAR.

BY THE END OF THE 1882 SEASON, SEVERAL HUNDREDS OF KILOMETERS OF TRACK HAD BEEN LAID. PEOPLE FINALLY BEGAN TO BELIEVE THAT THE RAILWAY WOULD BECOME A REALITY.

I NEVER BELIEVED I'D SEE A RAILWAY THIS FAR WEST!

I DIDN'T REALLY BELIEVE SIR JOHN MACDONALD COULD ACCOMPLISH THIS, BUT NOW I KNOW WE WILL ACTUALLY HAVE A TRANSCONTINENTAL RAILROAD, AND SOON!

IN SPITE OF THE ENORMOUS DIFFICULTIES AND CHALLENGES, WORK ON THE RAILWAY PROGRESSED BOTH EASTWARD AND WESTWARD.

IN 1884, LOCOMOTIVES BEGAN RUNNING BETWEEN YALE AND PORT MOODY.

I NEVER THOUGHT I'D SEE THIS DAY.

IN THE SPRING OF 1885, THE EASTERN PORTION OF TRACK WAS COMPLETED WITH THE CLOSING OF A GAP NEAR LAKE SUPERIOR.

THE EASTERN AND WESTERN PORTIONS OF THE TRACK WERE OFFICIALLY LINKED AT 9:25 A.M. ON NOVEMBER 7, 1885 IN CRAIGELLACHIE, BC WHEN SIR DONALD SMITH DROVE THE FINAL SPIKE IN THE RAILWAY.

THE RAILWAY WAS AN INCREDIBLE ENGINEERING FEAT. EQUALLY AMAZING WAS THAT IT TOOK LESS THAN 5 YEARS TO COMPLETE. AT 5,000 KILOMETERS IT WAS THE LONGEST RAILWAY ON EARTH. IT WAS 1,610 KILOMETERS LONGER THAN U.S. TRANSCONTINENTAL RAILWAY.

ALTHOUGH THE RAILWAY WAS OFFICIALLY COMPLETE, ITS STORY WAS FAR FROM OVER. THE ENTIRE COUNTRY WAS NOW LINKED BY A RAILROAD, BUT THE INTERIOR NEEDED TO BE SETTLED. THE CPR WAS NEARLY **BANKRUPT**, AND THE COMPANY NEEDED TO BEGIN MAKING A PROFIT. THE CPR DECIDED TO SELL THE FARMLAND IT HAD RECEIVED FOR THE CONTRACT. IF FARMERS BOUGHT THE LAND, THEY WOULD NEED THE RAILWAY TO SHIP THEIR CROPS.

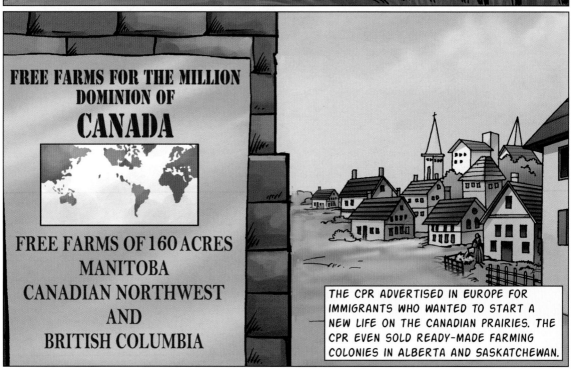

FREE FARMS FOR THE MILLION
DOMINION OF
CANADA

FREE FARMS OF 160 ACRES
MANITOBA
CANADIAN NORTHWEST
AND
BRITISH COLUMBIA

THE CPR ADVERTISED IN EUROPE FOR IMMIGRANTS WHO WANTED TO START A NEW LIFE ON THE CANADIAN PRAIRIES. THE CPR EVEN SOLD READY-MADE FARMING COLONIES IN ALBERTA AND SASKATCHEWAN.

WILLIAM VAN HORNE HAD ANOTHER IDEA FOR ENCOURAGING PEOPLE TO RIDE THE RAILWAY. HE BUILT THREE HOTELS AT ESPECIALLY SCENIC LOCATIONS. THESE HOTELS SERVED AS REST STATIONS FOR TRAVELERS.

I AM SO TIRED AND HUNGRY. WHAT A BEAUTIFUL PLACE TO STOP AND REST.

LATER, RESORTS AT SCENIC PLACES LIKE BANFF HOT SPRINGS AND LAKE LOUISE BROUGHT TOURISTS AND TRADE TO THE WEST.

BANFF NATIONAL PARK
Canada's First National Park
Established 188

THOUSANDS OF PEOPLE CONTINUE TO TRAVEL ON THE CANADIAN PACIFIC RAILWAY, EXPERIENCING AN AMAZING ENGINEERING FEAT AND SEEING THE NATION'S GREAT BEAUTY, VASTNESS, AND DIVERSITY.

Brain Teasers

1. Why did British Columbia insist on a transcontinental railroad?

2. How was Sir John Macdonald's vision of a transcontinental railway different than Alexander Mackenzie's vision?

3. Why did it take a whole year of work before Andrew Onderdonk began laying track in British Columbia?

4. Why did Andrew Onderdonk bring in Chinese laborers?

5. What were two difficulties railroad contractors faced in the muskeg?

6. Why did the CPR need farmers to settle the land along the railway?

7. Why was the last spike driven into track in British Columbia rather than in Ontario?

Answers

1. The province was isolated and needed to be linked with the rest of the country.

2. Macdonald felt that a complete railway stretching from the East to the West was a government priority for drawing the nation together. Mackenzie felt that private companies, not the government, should build the railroad and that it did not need to be a complete railway stretching from the East to the West.

3. Andrew Onderdonk had to prepare the passage through the mountains before he could begin laying track. This meant blasting away the rock walls of the canyon to provide a level surface for the track.

4. Andrew Onderdonk needed more workers than were available in British Columbia.

5. Workers in the muskeg faced terrain that did not support tracks so the swamp had to be cleared, filled, or trestles built over it. Workers also battled mosquitoes and black flies.

6. Unless farmers filled in the prairies, the CPR would have very little business. They needed farmers buying supplies and selling produce, all of which would be shipped by train.

7. The track was not built in one long stretch from east to west or west to east. It was built from both directions and the two sides met in British Columbia.

Further Information

How can I find out more about the transcontinental railroad?

Most libraries have computers that connect to a database that contains information on books and articles about different subjects. You can input a key word and find material on the person, place, or thing you want to learn more about. The computer will provide you with a list of books in the library that contain information on the subject you searched for. Non-fiction books are arranged numerically, using their call numbers. Fiction books are organized alphabetically by the author's last name.

Books

Berton, Pierre. *The Last Spike: The Great Railway, 1881–1885*. Anchor Canada, 2001.

Berton, Pierre. *The National Dream: The Great Railway, 1871–1881*. Anchor Canada, 2001.

Den Otter, A.A. *The Philosophy of Railways: The Transcontinental Railway Idea in British North America*. University of Toronto Press, 1997.

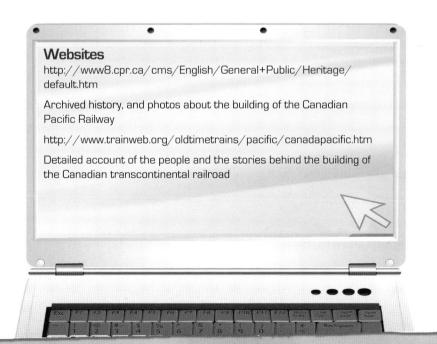

Websites
http://www8.cpr.ca/cms/English/General+Public/Heritage/default.htm

Archived history, and photos about the building of the Canadian Pacific Railway

http://www.trainweb.org/oldtimetrains/pacific/canadapacific.htm

Detailed account of the people and the stories behind the building of the Canadian transcontinental railroad

Glossary

bankrupt: financially ruined; unable to pay the debts owed to others

bedrock: solid rock that lies below the soil

depression: a poor economic condition when business activities are very slow and many people are out of work

incorporated: formed into a legal business corporation

monopoly: complete control over an industry by a single company or person

muskeg: a very thick swamp or bog

nitroglycerine: an explosive, poisonous liquid used to make dynamite

Pacific Scandal: In April 1873, Prime Minister John A. Macdonald was accused of taking campaign funds from Sir Hugh Allan in exchange for awarding Allan's group the contract to build the Canadian Pacific Railway. Macdonald's government was forced to resign because of the scandal, and in the next general election, the Conservative party was defeated by the Liberals.

predecessor: one who comes before another in time; a person who held a particular office before the current officeholder

ring bolt: a heavy metal rod used to fasten things together; it has a looped head and a ring on one end that is used to attach cables and ropes

Rupert's Land: Named in honor of Prince Rupert, the first governor of the Hudson's Bay Company and King Charles II's cousin, Rupert's Land encompassed the entire drainage basin of the Hudson Bay. In current-day terms, this includes northern Québec and Ontario north of the Laurentian watershed, all of Manitoba, most of Saskatchewan, southern Alberta, and a portion of the Northwest Territories and Nunavut. The Hudson's Bay Company was to have total control of this vast territory.

security: money or other goods given to assure the fulfillment of an obligation or promise

spike: a large, heavy nail that is used to attach the rails to the railroad ties in the track

whirlpool: a current of water that rotates very quickly in a circle

Index